Owls, Bats Wolves
and Othe 𝐼𝐷𝐸𝑆𝑂𝐼𝑇𝑆 *nals*

By Kris Hirschmann

World Discovery Science Readers™

SCHOLASTIC INC.

New York • Toronto • London • Auckland • Sydney
Mexico City • New Delhi • Hong Kong • Buenos Aires

Chapter 1

The Night Life

Many animals go to sleep when the sun sets. Their day is over. But other animals wake up when night falls. Their day is just starting.

Animals that are active during the day are called **diurnal** animals. Animals that are active at night are called **nocturnal** animals.

People are diurnal. We do not usually see night animals, since we are active during the daytime. More animals are nocturnal than diurnal. The night is alive with the movement and sounds of nocturnal creatures.

Why are some animals nocturnal instead of diurnal?

Some animals feel safer at night. Rabbits roam at night to avoid dogs, hawks, buzzards, and other diurnal hunters. These daytime **predators** are dangerous to rabbits.

But many night animals are dangerous to rabbits, too. Cats, badgers, weasels, and other night predators eat rabbits. So rabbits are most active just before dark and early in the morning.

Rabbits are gentle creatures. They do not have sharp claws, long teeth, or other weapons to protect themselves. Rabbits stay close to home. They run for safety if a predator comes near.

About ninety percent of all rabbits are killed by predators during their first year of life. A very lucky rabbit might live to be three years old.

A running rabbit flashes the white underside of its tail to warn other rabbits of danger. This white underside is called a **scut**.

Some animals hunt at night. Lynx are night hunters. Lynx are big cats that live in Europe, Asia, and North America. They eat rabbits, hares, birds, small deer, and other nocturnal animals.

Lynx have excellent vision and hearing. They use these senses to find prey at night. Lynx hunt by sneaking up on prey. They pounce when they get close enough.

Lynx have short tails and patches of black hair on their ear tips. These features make the lynx easy to recognize.

Tarantulas are night hunters, too. These big spiders live in deserts. Their bodies have hard coverings called **exoskeletons**. The sun's rays can heat up the exoskeleton, just like a car heats up on a summer day.

Tarantulas hunt at night, when the desert is cool. They eat insects, lizards, and mice. A tarantula sits very still and lets prey get near. Then, it jumps out and bites the prey with its sharp fangs. The fangs pump **venom** into the prey. The venom turns the prey's insides to mush. Then the tarantula drinks the prey's liquidy insides.

Tree frogs come out at night to avoid the sun. Water enters and leaves the frog's body through the skin. The hot sun would dry up the frog's skin. This would kill the frog.

There are about four hundred types of tree frogs. Most of them live near water or in rain forests. Tree frogs choose damp homes for the same reason they stay out of the sun: to keep their skin moist.

Some types of tree frogs use air sacs in their throats to make loud noises. They often sing at night when rain is coming, so some people call them "rain frogs."

The sun dries things through **evaporation**. The sun's heat turns water into vapor. The vapor floats away into the air.

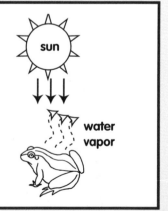

Chapter 2

Night Senses

Most day creatures depend on their vision. This makes sense when the sun is up and the world is bright. But everything is dark at night. It is not easy to see.

Nocturnal animals solve this problem in different ways. Some animals have special eyes that let them see well even at night. Others use hearing, touch, or smell to help them get around.

Many nocturnal animals have slit pupils. Slit pupils 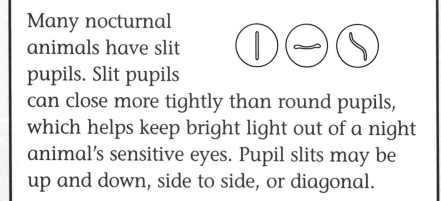 can close more tightly than round pupils, which helps keep bright light out of a night animal's sensitive eyes. Pupil slits may be up and down, side to side, or diagonal.

Owls can see well, even on the darkest night. An owl's eyes are so big that they cannot move inside its head. An owl has to turn its head if it wants to look to the side.

Owls fly quietly and look for mice, snakes, and other prey on the ground. They swoop down and grab the prey with sharp claws called talons.

An owl eats its prey whole. Then it spits out a ball of bones and anything else its body cannot use. This ball is called an owl pellet.

Some nocturnal animals' eyes seem to glow in the dark. They glow when light bounces off a shiny layer at the back of the eyes. This layer is called the **tapetum.**

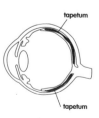

tapetum

tapetum

Bats use sound to help them get around. Bats make clicking sounds as they fly. These sounds bounce off things and **echo** back to the bat's ears. This process is called **echolocation**. The echoes tell the bat when something is in its way. They also help the bat to find things to eat.

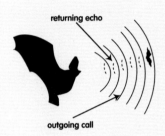

returning echo

outgoing call

Insects, frogs, and other prey can hear a bat's calls. They sometimes hide when they hear a bat coming.

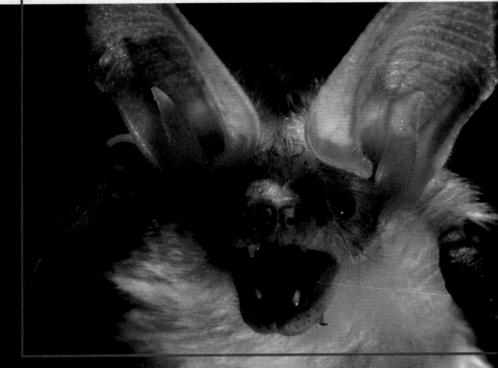

Animals leave tracks in mud, snow, and other soft surfaces. A raccoon's track has a distinct shape.

paw

track

Raccoons have a good sense of touch. They use their front paws to feel things in the dark. The front paws have five fingers. Each finger ends in a sharp claw.

Raccoons are good climbers. They use their sensitive paws to feel their way up trees. They can come down either headfirst or tailfirst.

Raccoons also use their paws to grab fish, nuts, berries, and other things to eat. They can even open doors, refrigerators, and garbage cans to get food.

Hedgehogs like strong smells. Hedgehogs foam at the mouth when they smell something they like.  They mix the smell into the foam and spread the smelly foam all over their bodies. This is called **self-anointing**. A hedgehog may self-anoint to make itself smell bad to predators.

Hedgehogs have about five thousand spines that protect them. A hedgehog rolls its body into a ball to make the spines stick out. The tighter the hedgehog curls, the spikier it gets. Any animal that bites the hedgehog will get poked in the mouth!

Hedgehogs' spines are round under the skin. This keeps hedgehogs from poking themselves.

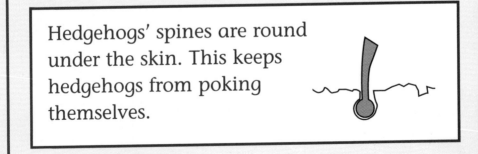

Chapter 3

Night Communication

The night is full of animal sounds. Frogs croak to one another, crickets chirp, and owls hoot. Raccoons chatter and mice squeak. These nighttime animals are communicating through sound.

Nocturnal creatures may also **communicate** without sound. Animals can use smell, light, and color to find others of their kind.

Humans are the only creatures on Earth that use spoken **language** (sounds that stand for specific things). Other creatures use sound to communicate feelings, location, mood, and other general ideas.

Wolves communicate by howling.
A wolf howls to find its **pack**. Packs are groups of wolves that live together. The pack howls back when a lost wolf is trying to find its way home.

Wolves also howl for safety. Wolves from different packs sometimes fight one another. Packs will howl together to scare away strange wolves. The howls echo off trees and cliffs and make the pack sound bigger than it really is.

The leader of a wolf pack is called the alpha male. The alpha male is the largest and strongest wolf in the pack. He howls more than the other wolves.

Wolves also communicate with body language. Here are three wolf postures and their meanings.

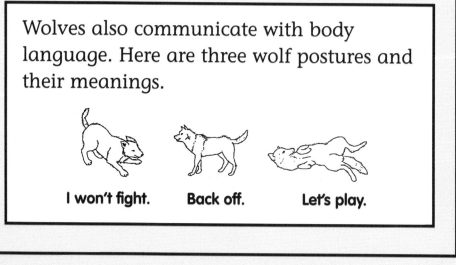

I won't fight.   **Back off.**   **Let's play.**

Skunks use smell to communicate. They spray a stinky liquid from two **glands** under their tails. This liquid is called **scent**. Skunks use scent to mark their home areas and to attract other skunks.

Skunks also spray to defend themselves. They squirt their scent into predators' faces. The spray makes animals feel sick. It also makes their eyes and noses hurt. Skunks can squirt their scent about 12 feet (3.7 m).

Sometimes people get sprayed by skunks. They have to take baths in tomato juice to make the smell go away.

Fireflies communicate with light.
Fireflies make light when two **chemicals**
mix inside their bodies. The chemicals
are called **luciferin** and **luciferase**.

Male fireflies turn their lights on and
off to attract females. Different types of
fireflies flash in different ways. A female
firefly only goes to a male if he is flashing
the right pattern.

Sometimes fireflies copy the blinking
patterns of different species. When they
do this, they attract different kinds of
fireflies. Then they eat them.

Badgers have bold colors that let them see one another in the dark. These night animals have black-and-white stripes on their faces. The white stripes stand out at night. Badgers can recognize other badgers by the shapes of their stripes.

Badgers can also recognize one another by smell. Badgers can smell hundreds of times better than humans can smell.

A badger's front legs are strong. It has long claws. A badger uses its claws to dig up the nests of rabbits, mice, and other prey.

Badgers have sharp front teeth for biting and tearing. Their back teeth are flat for grinding.

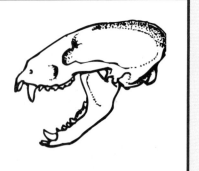

Chapter 4

Daytime Homes

Nocturnal animals go to sleep when the sun comes up. They are tired after a busy night. They will rest all day long.

Most night animals hide while they rest. They do not want to be found by diurnal predators.

Where do night creatures go during the daytime?

Scientists sometimes attach tiny radio transmitters to night animals. These radios send out signals so scientists can find the animals' daytime homes.

Some bats fly into dark caves. They hang upside down from the ceiling to rest. A bat's daytime home is called a **roost**. Sometimes millions of bats roost together in the same cave.

A group of bats that roosts together is called a **colony**. Mexican free-tailed bats form the biggest colonies. These bats fly from their roosts in one large group when night falls. They spend the night looking for bugs to eat.

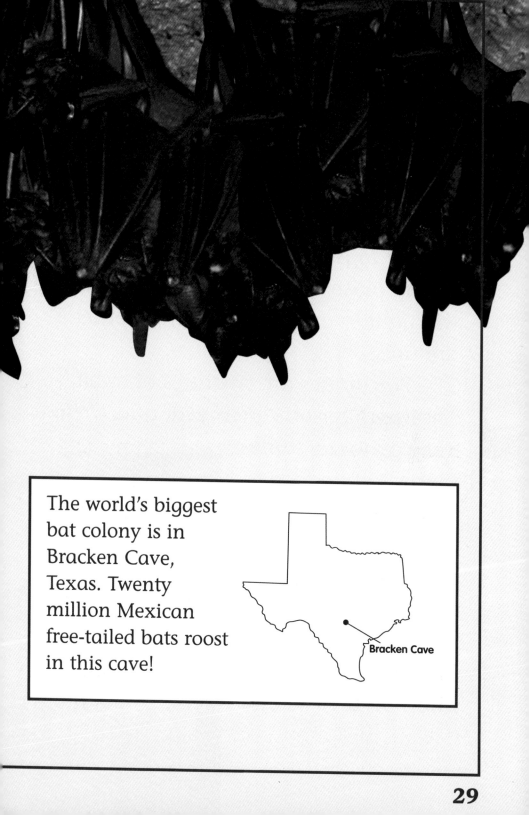

The world's biggest bat colony is in Bracken Cave, Texas. Twenty million Mexican free-tailed bats roost in this cave!

Bracken Cave

A porcupine's **quills** are covered with tiny backward-pointing spikes. The spikes make the quills hard to pull out if they are poked into an animal's flesh.

During the day, porcupines hide in hollow logs or tree trunks. A porcupine's hiding place is called a **den**. A porcupine will fight to protect its den from other animals.

Porcupines are creatures of habit. They use the same dens year after year. They go to the same places to find food every night.

A porcupine protects itself with sharp spikes called quills. Porcupines have up to 30,000 quills on their bodies.

Mice share human homes when the sun is up. These night animals often hide inside people's  walls, basements, and attics. They steal paper and shred it to make nests.

Mice can squeeze through gaps as narrow as one-quarter inch (6 mm). This makes it hard to keep them out of houses. Mice start having babies as soon as they settle in a house. One mouse can have up to sixty babies in a year!

All of these babies will wake up each night after the sun goes down. So will the world's bats, owls, wolves, badgers, and other nocturnal creatures. Most of the world does not go to sleep when you do. Millions upon millions of animals are starting their day just as you are going to bed.

Glossary

Chemicals—The basic building blocks of all matter. Everything is made of chemicals.

Colony—A group of bats that live together.

Communicate—To share ideas or information.

Den—The name given to some animals' homes.

Diurnal (die-URN-ull)—Active during the daytime.

Echo—A sound that bounces off something and returns.

Echolocation (ECK-oh-lo-KAY-shun)—Using sound to sense objects.

Evaporation—When a liquid turns into vapor.

Exoskeleton—A hard outer covering that some insects have.

Glands—In skunks, organs that produce scent.

Language—Systems of words that stand for specific ideas.

Luciferase (loo-SIF-er-ays)—A light-producing chemical in a firefly's body.

Luciferin (loo-SIF-er-in)—Another light-producing chemical in a firefly's body.

Nocturnal—Active during the night.

Pack—A family group of wolves.

Predators—Animals that hunt and eat other animals.

Quills—The sharp spikes of a porcupine.

Roost—A place where bats rest during the daytime.

Scent—The smelly liquid made by skunks and other animals.

Scut—The white underside of a rabbit's tail.

Self-anointing—Covering itself with foam.

Tapetum—A layer at the back of some animals' eyes that reflects light.

Venom—Poisonous liquid that an animal uses to kill prey or protect itself.